This Is What I Want to Be

Nurse

Heather Miller

Heinemann Library
Chicago, Illinois

©2003 Reed Educational & Professional Publishing
Published by Heinemann Library,
an imprint of Reed Educational & Professional Publishing
Chicago, IL

Customer Service 888-454-2279
Visit our website at www.heinemannlibrary.com

Designed by Sue Emerson, Heinemann Library
Printed and bound in the United States by Lake Book Manufacturing, Inc.

07 06 05 04 03
10 9 8 7 6 5 4 3 2 1

Library of Congress Cataloging-in-Publication Data
Miller, Heather.
    Nurse / Heather Miller.
      p. cm. — (This is what I want to be)
Includes index.
    ISBN: 1-4034-0370-8 (HC), 1-4034-0592-1 (Pbk.)
    1. Nursing—Juvenile literature. [1. Nursing. 2. Occupations.] I. Title.
    RT61.5 .M53 2002
    610.73'06'9—dc21

                          2001008137

Acknowledgments
The author and publishers are grateful to the following for permission to reproduce copyright material:
p. 4 Keith Brofsky/PhotoDisc; p. 5 Pete Saloutos/Corbis Stock Market; p. 6 Richard Price/FPG International; p. 7 Arthur Tilley/FPG International; pp. 8, 9, 14 Corbis Stock Market; p. 10L Frank Siteman/Mira.com; p. 10R Novastock/ International Stock; p. 11L Keith Brofsky/PhotoDisc/Getty Images; p. 11R Michael Keller/Corbis Stock Market; pp. 12, 16 Adam Smith/FPG International; p. 13 David Buffington/PhotoDisc; p. 15 Andy Levin/Photo Researchers, Inc.; p. 17 V. C. L./FPG International; p. 17 Susie Leavines/Photo Researchers, Inc.; p. 18L Tommy Ewasko/The Image Bank/Getty Images; p. 18R Andersen Ross/PhotoDisc; p. 19 David Joel/Stone/Getty Images; p. 20 Charles Gupton/Corbis Stock Market; p. 21 Bill Horsman/Stock Boston; p. 23 (row 1, L-R) Bernardo Bucci/Corbis Stock Market, C Squared Studios/PhotoDisc, EyeWire Collection, Corbis Stock Market; p. 23 (row 2, L-R) Corbis Stock Market, Corbis Stock Market, Keith Brofsky/PhotoDisc, Comstock Images; p. 23 (row 3, L-R) Eric Fowke/PhotoEdit, David Joel/Stone/Getty Images, Corbis Stock Market, Corbis Stock Market; p. 23 (row 4) Science Photo Library/Photo Researchers, Inc.

Cover photograph by Ron Chapple/FPG International
Photo research by Scott Braut

Every effort has been made to contact copyright holders of any material reproduced in this book. Any omissions will be rectified in subsequent printings if notice is given to the publisher.

Special thanks to our advisory panel for their help in the preparation of this book:

Eileen Day, Preschool Teacher
Chicago, IL

Ellen Dolmetsch, MLS
Wilmington, DE

Kathleen Gilbert,
Second Grade Teacher
Austin, TX

Sandra Gilbert,
Library Media Specialist
Houston, TX

Angela Leeper,
Educational Consultant
North Carolina Department
of Public Instruction
Raleigh, NC

Pam McDonald, Reading Teacher
Winter Springs, FL

Melinda Murphy,
Library Media Specialist
Houston, TX

We would also like to thank Michelle Schaffner, R.N., of Stanford University Hospital for her
help in the preparation of this book.

Some words are shown in bold, **like this.**
You can find them in the picture glossary on page 23.

Contents

What Do Nurses Do?

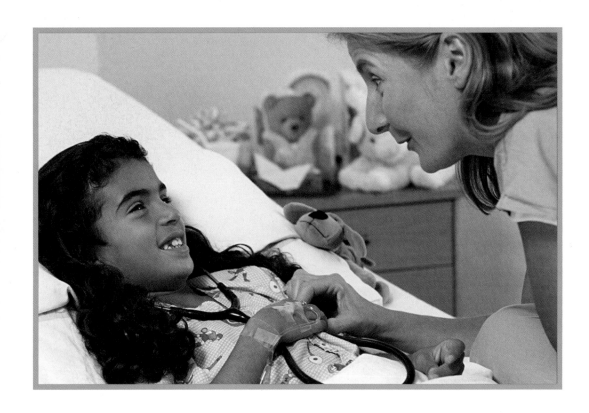

Nurses care for people.

They help people who are sick or hurt.

Nurses work with doctors.

Nurses teach people how to stay healthy.

What Is a Nurse's Day Like?

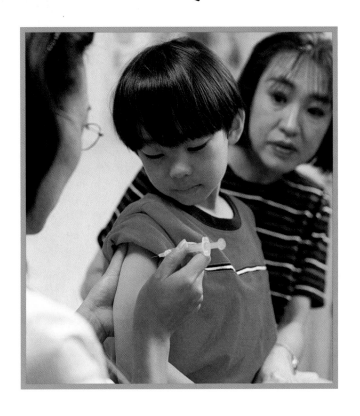

Nurses see many **patients** each day.

They give people shots or **medicine.**

They take care of sick and healthy people.

Sometimes nurses give patients treats!

What Do Nurses Wear?

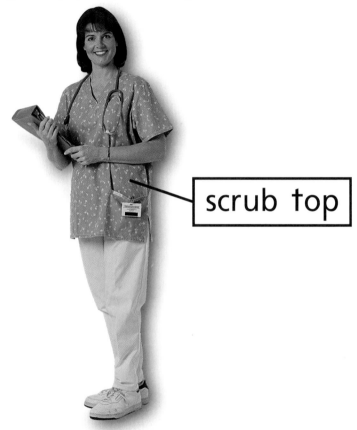

scrub top

Many nurses wear **scrub tops.**

Scrub tops may be white or bright colors.

name tag

Nurses wear **name tags** to tell people who they are.

Nurses often wear white shoes.

What Tools Do Nurses Use?

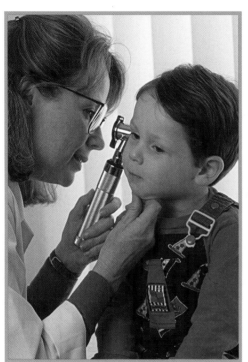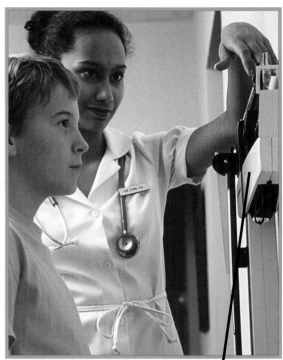

scale

Sometimes, nurses use an **otoscope** to check people's ears.

They use a **scale** to find out how much people weigh.

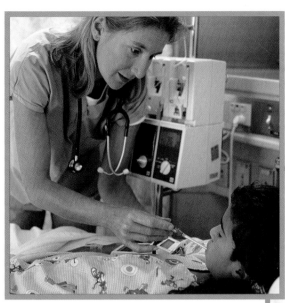

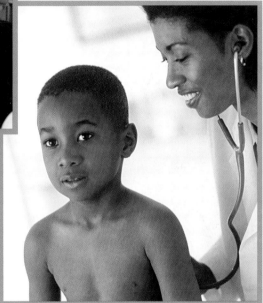

Nurses use a **thermometer** to check for a fever.

This nurse listens to a boy's **lungs** with a **stethoscope.**

Where Do Nurses Work?

Some nurses work in a doctor's office.

Others work in **hospitals.**

Nurses also work in schools.

They help children who are sick or hurt.

Do Nurses Work in Other Places?

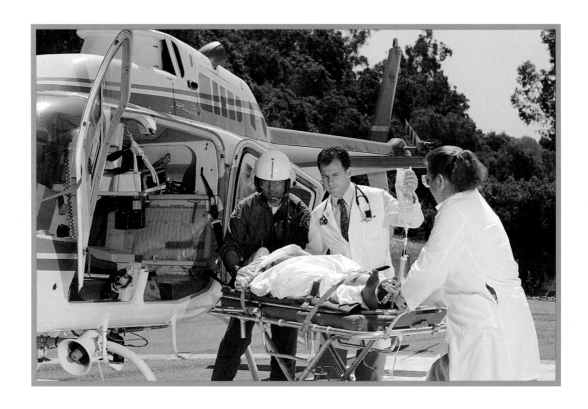

Some nurses fly in **helicopters**.

They help people who are badly hurt.

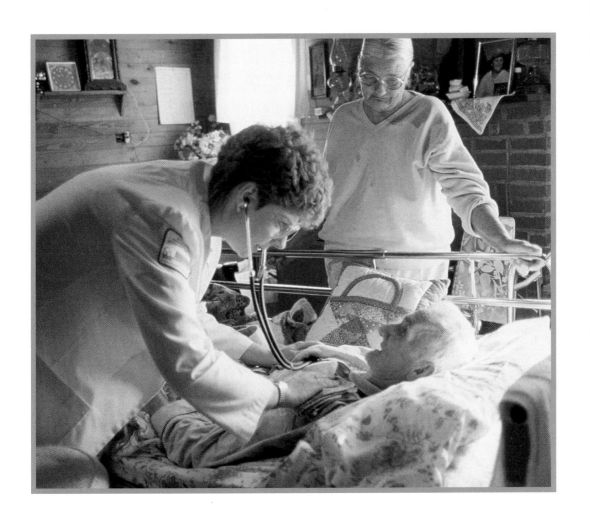

Some nurses help people in their homes.

They may visit many people each day.

When Do Nurses Work?

There are nurses working every day of the week.

Some nurses work during the day.

Other nurses work at night.

Nurses work on holidays, too.

What Kinds of Nurses Are There?

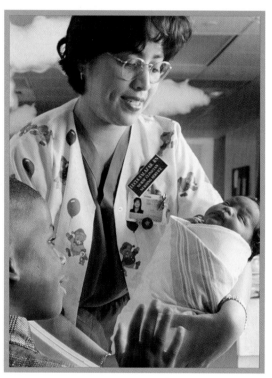

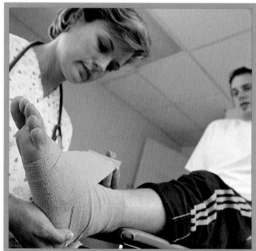

Some nurses take care of new babies in the **hospital**.

Other nurses help in the **emergency room**.

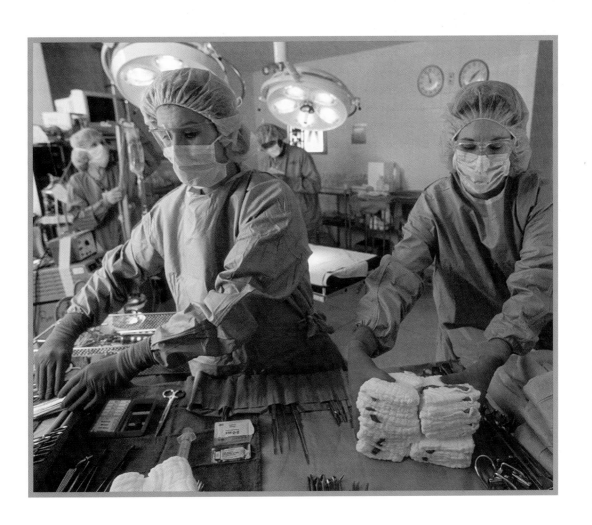

Some nurses help in **operating rooms.**

They help doctors with the tools they need.

How Do People Become Nurses?

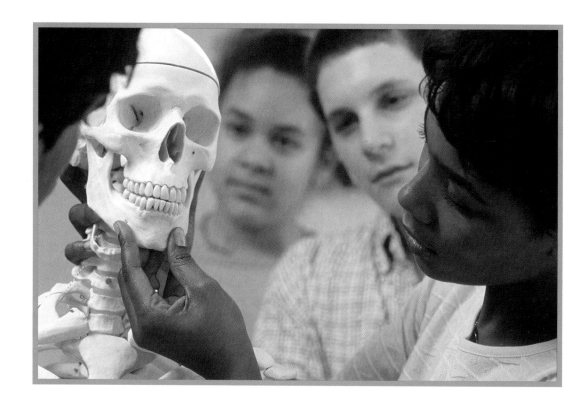

People go to college or nursing school to become nurses.

They study math and science.

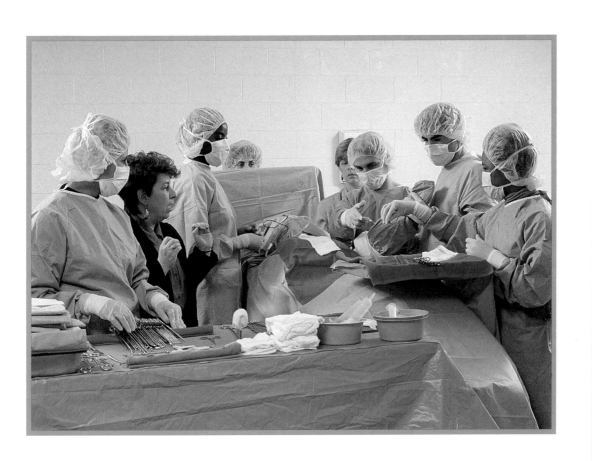

They spend time in **hospitals.**

They learn how people's
bodies work.

Quiz

Can you remember what these things are called?

Look for the answers on page 24.

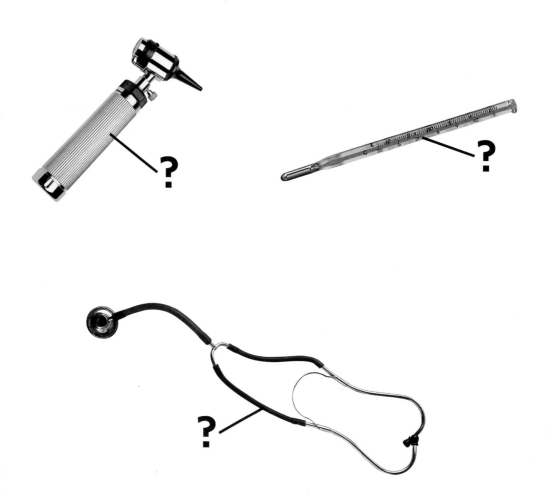

Picture Glossary

emergency room
page 18

medicine
page 6

otoscope
page 10

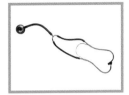

scrub top
page 8

helicopter
page 14

name tag
page 9

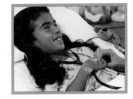

patient
pages 6, 7

stethoscope
page 11

hospital
pages 12,
18, 21

operating room
page 19

scale
page 10

thermometer
page 11

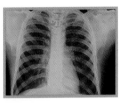

lungs
page 11

Note to Parents and Teachers

Reading for information is an important part of a child's literacy development. Learning begins with a question about something. Help children think of themselves as investigators and researchers by encouraging their questions about the world around them. Each chapter in this book begins with a question. Read the question together. Look at the pictures. Talk about what you think the answer might be. Then read the text to find out if your predictions were correct. Think of other questions you could ask about the topic, and discuss where you might find the answers. Assist children in using the picture glossary and the index to practice new vocabulary and research skills.

Index

Answers to quiz on page 22

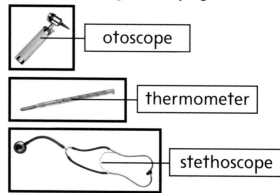

otoscope

thermometer

stethoscope